To:

_____

From:

_____

Date:

_____

Copyright © 2011 by Christian Art Kids, an imprint of Christian Art Publishers, PO Box 1599, Vereeniging, 1930, RSA

1025 N Lombard Road, Lombard, IL, 60148, USA

First edition 2011

Cover designed by Christian Art Kids

Images used under license from Shutterstock.com

Set in 16 on 20 pt Chalkboard by Christian Art Kids

Printed in China

ISBN 978-1-77036-729-6

11 12 13 14 15 16 17 18 19 20 – 10 9 8 7 6 5 4 3 2 1

Prayers for
Little Hearts

Carolyn Larsen

I start my day with prayer

Dear God, thank You for a restful night.
And thank You for a new day's light.
Thank You that I can start this day
by taking time to simply pray.

Amen.

Each morning I pray to You, LORD.
Psalm 88:13

Playtime is fun!

Dear God, do You like to watch me play?
I hope so 'cause I play all day.
You made a lot of fun things for me to do.
And for that I say a big THANK YOU.

Amen.

Give thanks to the LORD, for He is good;
His love endures forever.
1 Chronicles 16:34

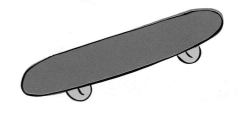

Good friends

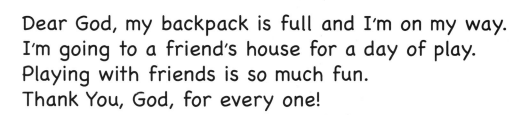

Dear God, my backpack is full and I'm on my way.
I'm going to a friend's house for a day of play.
Playing with friends is so much fun.
Thank You, God, for every one!

Amen.

I choose as my friends everyone who
worships You and follows Your teachings.
Psalm 119:63

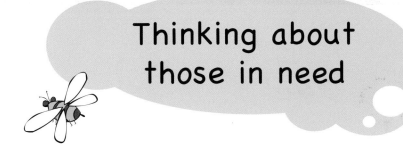

Thinking about those in need

Dear God, reading is one thing I love to do.
Every book teaches me something new.
I know some kids have no books to read.
Help me find a way to meet their need.

Amen.

Children, you show love for others by truly helping them, and not merely by talking about it.
1 John 3:18

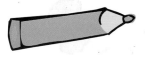

My dog is my best friend

Dear God, I love to play with my dog, Joe.
He follows me everywhere I go.
Thank You for giving Joe to me.
He makes life more fun than I thought it could be.

Amen.

Good people are kind to their animals.
Proverbs 12:10

God's wonderful gifts

Dear God, I know that You made everything.
Butterflies, bunnies and birds that sing.
You made lots of flowers, some purple some blue,
and for them all, I give praise to You!

Amen.

In the beginning God created the heavens and the earth.
Genesis 1:1

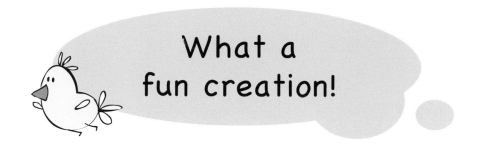

What a fun creation!

Dear God, was it fun to think up things to make?
Like oceans, rivers, streams and lakes
and lambs and birds and flowers and bees.
Thank You for making these things for me!

Amen.

The earth is the LORD's, and everything in it.
Psalm 24:1

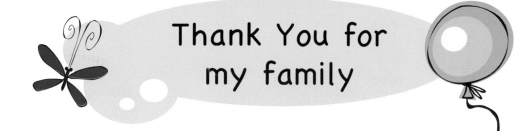

Thank You for my family

Dear God, sometimes brothers are not much fun.
Sometimes sisters make you run.
But I have to say something that just can't wait ...
I'm thankful for my family; they are really great!

Amen.

Respect your father and mother.
And love others as much as you love yourself.
Matthew 19:19

Bursting with joy

Dear God, sometimes I feel so happy
I don't know what to do.
I want to sing and shout
about how much I love You!
I want to stand on a hilltop
and shout it loud and clear.
I want to shout it out so loud
that everyone can hear!

Amen.

I thank You from my heart, and I will never
stop singing Your praises, my LORD and my God.
Psalm 30:12

My favorite Book

Dear God, the Bible is my favorite Book
because it's all about You.
I like to read the stories
about all the things You do.
Thank You for the lessons
that teach me how to live,
and that I should help others
by being willing to give.

Amen.

Your word is a lamp to my feet
and a light for my path.
Psalm 119:105

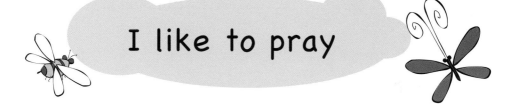

I like to pray

Dear God, thank You
that I can talk to You every single day.
Thank You for listening
to every prayer I pray.
I know that You are with me
wherever I may go.
So I can tell You anything
'cause You already know!

                    Amen.

Let's praise God! He listened when I prayed,
and He is always kind. Psalm 66:20

My favorite time of day

Dear God, first thing in the morning
is my favorite time of day.
We have breakfast together,
then we talk and pray.
I know my family loves me
and that they love You, too.
It's good to start our day this way,
by giving it to You!

Amen.

Each morning let me learn more
about Your love because I trust You.
Psalm 143:8

When I am feeling sick

Dear God, my head hurts.
My throat is sore. I feel pretty bad.
People take good care of me,
especially Mom and Dad.
Thank You for Your healing power
that will get me through this day.
You'll help me to feel better
so I can meet my friends and play.

Amen.

God heals the brokenhearted and binds
up their wounds. Psalm 147:3

My grandpa

Dear God, I love to stay at Grandpa's house
'cause I think he is the best.
He reads to me and plays games with me
and then I take a rest.
My grandpa tells me all about You.
He knows You pretty well.
My grandpa is terrific ...
in case You couldn't tell.

Amen.

Young people take pride in their strength,
but the gray hairs of wisdom
are even more beautiful.
Proverbs 20:29

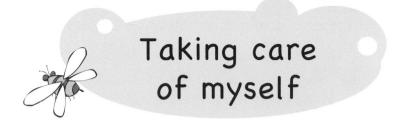

Taking care of myself

Dear God, Mom says my body is a temple
but I'm not sure what that means.
I think it means I have to choose
between junk and healthy things.
So, even if I'd rather have cake
I will choose some yummy fruit.
I promise to take care of myself —
being healthy will be the proof.

Amen.

Don't you know that you yourselves
are God's temple and that God's Spirit
lives in you? 1 Corinthians 3:16

Everyone is different

Dear God, everyone is different
and that is really fun.
Some like kittens, some like dogs
and some like either one.
I like that we are different
but still can all be friends.
Thank You for making everyone —
boys, girls, women and men!

Amen.

We are God's masterpiece. He has created us
anew in Christ Jesus, so we can do the good
things He planned for us long ago. Ephesians 2:10

Thinking of others

Dear God, some people think only
of themselves and that is pretty sad.
It's nice to notice others
when they are feeling bad.
Even when I am not happy,
help me to see who might feel worse.
Then show me how to be the one
who thinks of others first.

Amen.

Two are better than one, because they have a good
return for their work: If one falls down, his friend
can help him up. Ecclesiastes 4:9-10

Show your love

Dear God, it doesn't do any good
to love someone unless you let them know.
Love that is hidden isn't love,
it really has to show.
Thank You for those who love me
and those that I love too.
Thank You that we show our love.
I know it comes from YOU!

Amen.

We know and rely on the love God has for us.
God is love. Whoever lives in love lives
in God, and God in him. 1 John 4:16

Forgiving others

Dear God, I am mad, I am mad!
I know it sounds real bad.
But my friend hurt my feelings
and made me feel sad.
He keeps saying he is sorry,
but I don't want to listen.
I really need You to help me forgive him.

Amen.

Forgive us for doing wrong,
as we forgive others. Matthew 6:12

Jesus loves us all

Dear God, the world is full of people
and You see all of us.
You see us when we are happy.
You see us when we fuss.
We know that You always love us,
no matter what we do.
And we can love each other
with love that comes from You!

Amen.

Let us continue to love one another,
for love comes from God. Anyone who
loves is a child of God and knows God.
1 John 4:7

Night, night

Dear God, I used to be quite crabby
'cause I was scared at night.
I always waited eagerly
for the morning light.
But now I know that You
are watching over me.
So I can go to sleep each night
and rest so peacefully.

Amen.

I will lie down and sleep in peace, for You alone,
O LORD, make me dwell in safety. Psalm 4:8

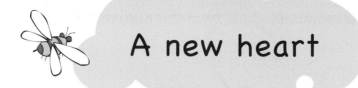

A new heart

Dear God, I gave away my heart today.
I gave it all to You.
Now everything seems different.
My heart feels so brand new.
Thank You for sending Jesus,
that shows Your amazing love.
Jesus is my Savior now
who came down from above.

Amen.

For God so loved the world that He
gave His one and only Son, that whoever
believes in Him shall not perish
but have eternal life. John 3:16